Vaccination Timeline

430 BCE

Ancient Greek doctors in Athens notice that people who have recovered from plague don't catch it again.

1346-1350

The Black Death kills up to half the population of Europe and parts of Asia.

1721

Lady Mary Wortley Montagu encourages variolation against smallpox in Britain.

10th Century CE

Chinese doctors use variolation to prevent smallpox.

1796

Edward Jenner vaccinates James Phipps.

1721

Cotton Mather tries variolation in America after hearing about it from a slave.

1924

Program to vaccinate against diphtheria in the United States begins.

1880s

Louis Pasteur discovers that vaccination protects people against rabies.

1980

World Health Organization (WHO) announces that smallpox has been wiped out by vaccination.

1918

Spanish flu kills more than 50 million people worldwide. Blood from recovered patients helps some sick people recover.

2000

WHO's target date for polio to be wiped out— but years later it is still present in a few countries.

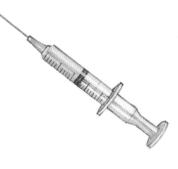

1955

Salk's polio vaccine is made generally available in the United States.

Vaccination Around the World

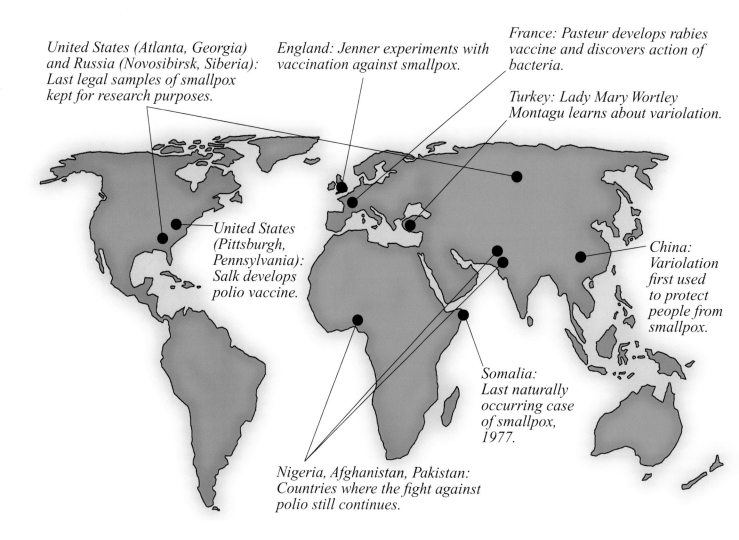

United States (Atlanta, Georgia) and Russia (Novosibirsk, Siberia): Last legal samples of smallpox kept for research purposes.

England: Jenner experiments with vaccination against smallpox.

France: Pasteur develops rabies vaccine and discovers action of bacteria.

Turkey: Lady Mary Wortley Montagu learns about variolation.

United States (Pittsburgh, Pennsylvania): Salk develops polio vaccine.

China: Variolation first used to protect people from smallpox.

Somalia: Last naturally occurring case of smallpox, 1977.

Nigeria, Afghanistan, Pakistan: Countries where the fight against polio still continues.

The struggle to conquer disease by vaccination has been fought worldwide. Medical progress has been made in many lands, and its benefits are felt everywhere.

The only way to eradicate a disease is to immunize people all over the world, so that a disease can't spring back from a small unvaccinated population.

Author:

Anne Rooney studied English at Cambridge University, England, and then earned a PhD at Cambridge. She has held teaching posts at several UK universities and is currently a Royal Literary Fund fellow at Newnham College, Cambridge. She has written more than 150 books for children and adults, including several on the history of science and medicine. She also writes children's fiction.

Artist:

David Antram was born in Brighton, England, in 1958. He studied at Eastbourne College of Art and then worked in advertising for 15 years before becoming a full-time artist. He has illustrated many children's nonfiction books.

Series creator:

David Salariya was born in Dundee, Scotland. He has illustrated a wide range of books and has created and designed many new series for publishers in the UK and overseas. David established The Salariya Book Company in 1989. He lives in Brighton, England, with his wife, illustrator Shirley Willis, and their son, Jonathan.

Editor: **Stephen Haynes**

Editorial Assistant: **Mark Williams**

Published in Great Britain in 2015 by
The Salariya Book Company Ltd
25 Marlborough Place, Brighton BN1 1UB

ISBN-13: 978-0-531-21366-7 (lib. bdg.) 978-0-531-21409-1 (pbk.)

All rights reserved.
Published in 2015 in the United States
by Franklin Watts
An imprint of Scholastic Inc.
Published simultaneously in Canada.

A CIP catalog record for this book is available
from the Library of Congress.

Printed and bound in China.
Printed on paper from sustainable sources.

1 2 3 4 5 6 7 8 9 10 R 24 23 22 21 20 19 18 17 16 15

PAPER FROM
SUSTAINABLE
FORESTS

You Wouldn't Want to Live Without™

Vaccinations!

Written by
Anne Rooney

Illustrated by
David Antram

Created and designed by
David Salariya

Franklin Watts®
An Imprint of Scholastic Inc.
NEW YORK • TORONTO • LONDON • AUCKLAND • SYDNEY
MEXICO CITY • NEW DELHI • HONG KONG
DANBURY, CONNECTICUT

Contents

Introduction

Sticking sharp needles into small children doesn't sound like a nice thing to do. But vaccination is definitely a case of being "cruel to be kind." The needle prick lasts only a moment, but in exchange you're protected against terrifying, deadly diseases that have killed millions of people in the past. That sounds like a fair swap, doesn't it?

Vaccination introduces a tiny amount of a safe version of a disease into the body. Your body's disease-fighting mechanisms spring into action to work out how to deal with the disease—only they don't actually need to, as it's not a real infection. But if you ever come into contact with the real disease, your body will know what to do. If you have been vaccinated against polio, or measles, or another disease, you won't become sick with it later. Your body recognizes the disease and can roll out its defenses before the disease gets a chance to take hold.

So, next time you have to get a shot, smile—it just might save your life!

It only hurts for a moment.

What Causes Disease?

We all get sick sometimes. Illness can be caused by the body failing in some way, or by infection caused by microorganisms. When we're sick, we have symptoms such as fever, vomiting, or suffering from aches, pains, coughs, and sniffles. Some symptoms are caused by the microorganisms themselves, but many are caused by things your body does as it fights the infection.

Most diseases are caused by bacteria or viruses. Some are caused by fungi or parasites. We already have vaccines to prevent infections caused by bacteria and viruses. Vaccines against parasites and fungal infections are being developed.

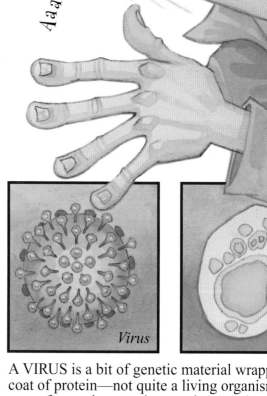

Aaa-choo!

Four Culprits

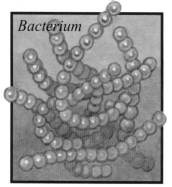

Bacterium

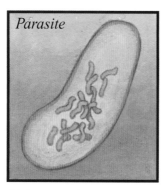

Parasite

Virus

Fungus

BACTERIA, PARASITES, AND FUNGI are all living organisms. There are more bacteria on the planet than any other type of organism. Parasites always live and feed in or on other organisms.

A VIRUS is a bit of genetic material wrapped in a coat of protein—not quite a living organism. Fungi range from microscopic organisms such as yeast to large mushrooms and toadstools.

BACTERIA are much larger than viruses. Bacteria were discovered first, as they are easy to see with a microscope. Viruses can be tiny—but just as deadly. Some bacteria are 100 times longer than viruses.

Bacterium

Virus

You Can Do It!

The best way of all to avoid infection is simple—wash your hands! Vaccination can protect you from many—but not all—serious diseases. Washing gets rid of bacteria and viruses on your skin before they have a chance to get inside your body.

DISEASES often spread from person to person through physical contact (touching). Coughs and sneezes spread diseases, too. Some are carried in body fluids, such as blood.

BACTERIA don't settle down with a mate and start a family. To reproduce, the bacterium makes a copy of its essential parts. One copy goes to each end of the bacterium, which splits in two.

DNA inside the cell copies itself.

The cell divides in two.

SOME INFECTIONS affect only part of the body. Others make the whole body sick.

VIRUSES need help to reproduce. They live inside a host cell, and hijack it to collect and copy the chemical bits and pieces they need to build copies of themselves. They turn cells into virus factories.

A virus injects its DNA into a cell.

Virus DNA and protein coats are made inside the cell.

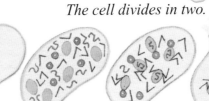

The viruses are put together.

The cell bursts and the viruses swarm out.

7

How the Body Fights Back

Your body is always on the lookout for invaders that might cause an infection. If it is threatened by bacteria or viruses that breach its defenses, it fights back. Your body's mechanism for fighting off infection is called the immune system.

At the first sign of trouble, the innate immune system launches its attack. It targets anything that shouldn't be there—it's what makes you sneeze if you breathe in dust, for example. To work, it needs to be able to recognize what's part of your body and what's not.

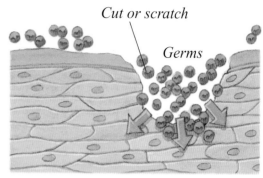

Cut or scratch

Germs

YOUR BODY'S very first line of defense is to keep germs out. You have a barrier all over your outside—your skin and your mucous membranes (the slimy layers inside your nose and mouth, for instance). A cut or scratch can let germs in, which is why we clean and cover wounds.

PHAGOCYTES are white blood cells that eat the invaders alive! They wrap themselves around the invader, making a little pocket to contain it. Then they inject chemicals to destroy it. This is part of the innate immune system.

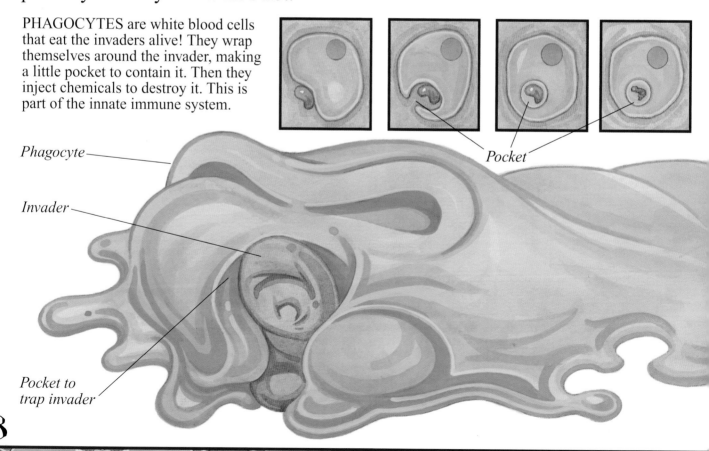

Pocket

Phagocyte

Invader

Pocket to trap invader

HEAT—fever, or a hot and swollen injury—is part of the innate immune system's response. Heat speeds up the immune system, and may kill some bacteria.

Top Tip

You don't always need to treat the fever that comes with illness. It might make you feel uncomfortable, but fever could be doing you good, helping your body to fight the germs. Always take your doctor's advice, though, as very high temperatures are dangerous.

WHEN A VIRUS infects body cells, the infected cells look just like normal ones, so phagoctyes leave them alone. Other white blood cells, called natural killer cells, find them, though. They bore holes in infected cells and inject chemicals to kill them.

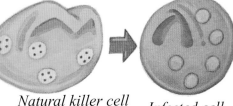

Natural killer cell   *Infected cell*

Dead cell

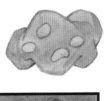

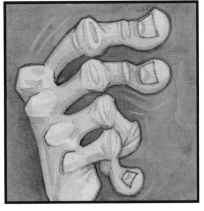

ALLERGIC REACTIONS to things like pollen and cats are caused by the immune system treating them as a threat.

RHEUMATOID ARTHRITIS is a very painful condition of the joints caused by the immune system not working right. The immune system attacks soft tissue in joints, destroying it as though it were invading cells.

TOO MUCH OF A GOOD THING. If the immune system works too hard at producing chemicals to fight infection, it can do more harm than good. Occasionally, it poisons the body and causes more serious illness.

Remembering the Enemy

The innate immune system is a good first response, but it treats all invaders the same —it's rather like lashing out at an attacker without looking for its weaknesses. Your body also has a slower response called adaptive immunity. It figures out how to fight each infection, and remembers each one. That means that it can respond quickly to the same infection in the future. This is what makes vaccination possible.

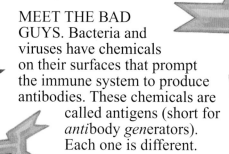

Antibodies

Virus

Antigens

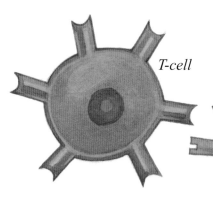

T-cell

B-cell

T-CELLS are white blood cells that tidy up the mess left by working antibodies, destroy virus-infected cells, and help remember antigens to recognize later.

B-CELLS are white blood cells with antibodies on their surface. When they find an antigen that matches an antibody, they turn into factories to produce lots of those antibodies.

MEET THE BAD GUYS. Bacteria and viruses have chemicals on their surfaces that prompt the immune system to produce antibodies. These chemicals are called antigens (short for *anti*body *gen*erators). Each one is different.

ANTIBODIES are the good guys. They're Y-shaped proteins with differently shaped ends that each fit onto a specific antigen. It's like fitting a key into a lock—you need the right antibody to fit each antigen.

NEWBORN BABIES already have immunity to some illnesses. They get this immunity from their mothers. For as long as babies are breast-fed, they are protected against infections that attack through the gut, such as those from germs that cause food poisoning. Babies slowly build their own immunity as they come into contact with more germs.

Top Tip

Make sure you get plenty of sleep and exercise and eat a healthy diet. It will all help to keep your immune system strong!

DOCTORS first noticed natural immunity during a plague in Athens, Greece, in 430 BCE. People who had survived the disease once didn't catch it again.

This is your first plague?

Variolation

How would you like to sniff up a load of crushed scabs from someone else's sores and pustules? No? Not before breakfast? It might save your life! In 10th-century China, and possibly in ancient Egypt, a doctor would put dried matter from smallpox sores into a patient's nose or into a scratch on their arm to protect them from smallpox. It's called variolation. The scabs carried some leftover smallpox virus—just enough to make the body produce antibodies that could protect the patient if they encountered smallpox later.

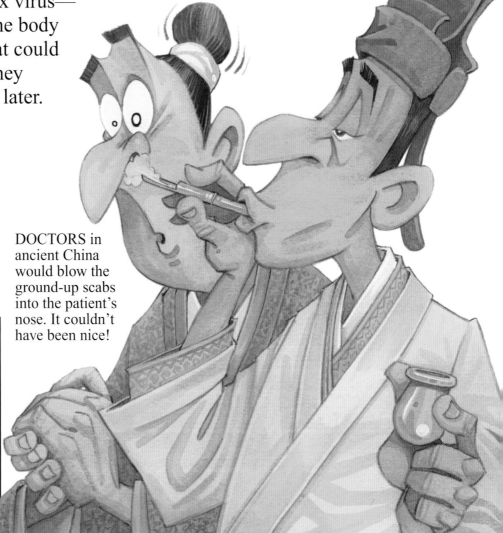

VARIOLATION spread around Asia, Africa, and India. Lady Mary Wortley Montagu saw it in Turkey and introduced the practice to England in 1721. She had survived smallpox herself and knew how awful it was.

DOCTORS in ancient China would blow the ground-up scabs into the patient's nose. It couldn't have been nice!

Variolation kills 1 in 50   *Smallpox kills 15 in 50*

How It Works

There's enough smallpox virus left in the dried scabs to jolt the body into producing antibodies to smallpox. The immune system remembers how to make these and can make lots later if needed.

We'd better get our shots up to date.

VARIOLATION was risky: 1 in 50 variolated people died of smallpox or another infection. But catching smallpox was even worse: 15 out of 50 people died.

SMALLPOX was a terrible disease that caused pain, fever, and a rash of pustules that looked like rice grains. Nearly a third of sufferers died. Many who recovered were left blind or brain damaged, and all were horribly scarred. Smallpox killed millions of people over thousands of years. It was finally wiped out in 1980 (see page 29).

THE OLDEST known smallpox victim is an Egyptian mummy. Pharaoh Ramesses V died of the disease in 1157 BCE, and the spots are still visible on his mummified body. Smallpox is probably at least 12,000 years old.

13

Vaccination

In 1796, British doctor Edward Jenner found a safer method than variolation. He knew that milkmaids rarely caught smallpox—but they often caught cowpox, a disease that causes nasty pustules on cows (and milkmaids) but is not dangerous. Thinking that perhaps cowpox protected the milkmaids from smallpox, he collected material from cowpox pustules, made a small cut on the arm of a young boy, James Phipps, and waited. Phipps didn't get cowpox. He didn't get smallpox either. Jenner's idea worked. Although people made fun of Jenner at first, vaccination became very popular. His invention has saved millions of lives.

JENNER TOOK PUS from the cowpox pustules on the hands and arms of a young milkmaid named Sarah Nelmes, to make his vaccine against smallpox.

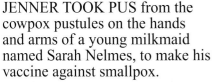

The body makes antibodies to the cowpox virus. The cowpox and smallpox viruses have some of the same antigens on the surface, so the cowpox antibodies fit and work against smallpox, too. If someone with cowpox antibodies is exposed to smallpox, they can make useful antibodies quickly.

Cowpox pustules

Cow's udders

A MILKMAID touches the cow's udders to milk the cow. If the cow has cowpox, she can catch it.

THE AMERICAN ARMY lost a battle for the control of Quebec, Canada, in 1775, when many of the soldiers caught smallpox. The victorious British army had been protected by variolation.

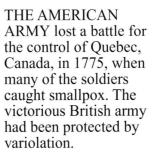

JENNER WASN'T THE FIRST to use cowpox to protect against smallpox. English farmer Benjamin Jesty vaccinated his wife and children with cowpox during a smallpox epidemic in 1774, but didn't tell people about it.

Pasteur's Happy Accident

Nearly 100 years after Jenner made his smallpox vaccine, French scientist Louis Pasteur was investigating diseases in animals. He told his assistant to inject some chickens with cholera bacteria that he had prepared. The assistant forgot. A month later, the assistant realized his mistake and gave the injection. The chickens became slightly sick, but got better. Pasteur tried giving them fresh cholera, but they were resistant to it. Pasteur realized he had accidentally discovered a vaccine—that leaving the cholera bacteria exposed to air had made them less powerful, but strong enough to protect his chickens.

Hold still! You'll thank me for this later.

Aaaark!

IN 1880, Pasteur started work on a vaccine to protect people from rabies, a deadly disease caught from animals. He used a glass tube to collect spit from a dog with rabies. Yikes!

PASTEUR made his rabies vaccine from the spinal cords of rabbits with rabies. He left the spinal cords to dry in the air so that the rabies was weakened and didn't cause the full-blown disease.

How It Works

Pasteur's vaccine could even save people who had already been bitten by a rabid animal, as long as they had not yet developed rabies—so they had to get to him quickly! The patient's body made antibodies to the vaccine, and could use these to fight off the real disease.

Just in time!

HE GAVE his rabies vaccine to people who had been bitten by rabid dogs, using one shot a day for 13 days. Patients who took all the doses survived, except one who started the course of treatment too late to be helped.

Timeline: The Discovery of Vaccination

1796: Jenner makes a smallpox vaccine.

1885: Pasteur makes a human rabies vaccine.

1921: First tuberculosis (TB) vaccine is developed.

1879: Pasteur discovers a vaccine for chicken cholera.

1895: Diphtheria vaccine to treat people who are already sick is made available in the United States.

How Vaccination Works

Both Jenner and Pasteur made effective vaccines without understanding how they worked. They protected people from terrible diseases, though, so everyone was happy.

Now, knowing how vaccination works helps us make better, safer vaccines. Vaccination introduces a tiny amount of a pathogen (something that causes a disease) to the body. The immune system figures out how to make antibodies that fit the disease's antigens, and remembers how to do it. If the same antigen comes along later, the immune system knows how to make the antibodies. It can combat the disease quickly, before an infection takes hold.

ARE YOU READY for your shot? It will hurt a tiny bit as the needle goes in, and your arm might be sore afterward. You might feel a little bit sick the next day. But after that you will be healthy, happy—and safe.

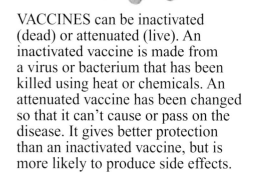

Inactivated virus

VACCINES can be inactivated (dead) or attenuated (live). An inactivated vaccine is made from a virus or bacterium that has been killed using heat or chemicals. An attenuated vaccine has been changed so that it can't cause or pass on the disease. It gives better protection than an inactivated vaccine, but is more likely to produce side effects.

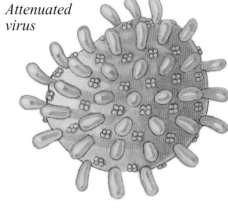

Attenuated virus

One child is vaccinated; the other refuses.

Both are exposed to the same pathogen.

IF SOMEONE is already sick, or has been exposed to a dangerous disease, he or she can be given antibodies directly. It's called passive immunization. A person bitten by a rabid dog is given antibodies to boost the body's immune system and fight rabies.

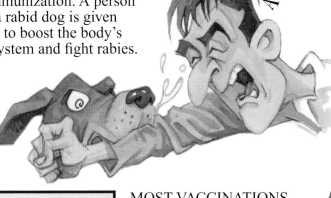

Aaaargh!

How It Works

Look closely—it's not scary. A hypodermic needle is hollow, with a slanted, pointy end to push easily through skin. The liquid vaccine in the barrel is pushed through the hollow needle when the nurse or doctor presses the plunger. Most needles are very thin.

Needle tip enlarged

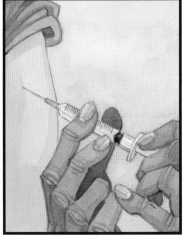

MOST VACCINATIONS are given as an injection. A doctor or nurse cleans your arm first. Then he or she uses the right amount of vaccine for you—smaller doses for smaller people—and a new, clean needle. They push the needle a little way into your arm, then press the plunger so the liquid flows through the needle. Then they press on your skin and pull the needle out. All done!

Is the Needle Really Necessary?

Many vaccines have to be injected because if you swallowed them they would be destroyed by the chemicals in your gut. But the vaccine for typhoid fever (a deadly disease passed on through infected food or water) is given by mouth, because it's tough—it's not harmed by stomach acid.

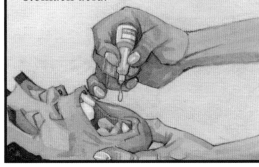

One child is protected; the other is not.

19

Diseases Are Best Avoided

Being a child in the early 1900s must have been scary and dangerous. Two deadly diseases, diphtheria and polio, claimed thousands of lives year after year. The first polio epidemic hit the United States in 1894. Epidemics became worse and worse. After 1916, there was one each year. Scientists raced to make a vaccine and at last they succeeded, defeating polio in the 1950s. Diphtheria affected 200,000 people a year until a vaccination program stopped it in its tracks in 1924.

POLIO is caused by a virus in dirty water. It attacks the nervous system. It makes muscles waste away, causing paralysis or death.

JONAS SALK released the first successful inactivated vaccine in 1955. It had been tested on young people in the United States in the largest medical trial in history. Mass immunization started, and polio cases fell by 90 percent—from 56,000 to 5,600—in a year.

AT THE SAME time, Albert Sabin was developing a live polio vaccine. It was ready in 1962. It worked better than Salk's and could be taken by mouth, which made it easier to give to people. Sabin's vaccine is still used in some parts of the world today.

THE VERY FIRST polio vaccine, made in 1950, was effective only for a few weeks. In 1952, the worst epidemic ever left 21,000 people paralyzed. In 1955, Salk announced his vaccine and people braved long lines to receive it.

You Can Do It!

It's important to make sure all your vaccinations are up to date. Some have to be given at intervals several years apart. Check your own vaccination records (you can get them from your doctor) to make sure you have had all your shots.

Mass of dead cells in throat

Antitoxin Delivery

An antitoxin to cure diphtheria was developed in 1895. To work, it had to be given quickly to people who had caught diphtheria. In the winter of 1925, a dramatic delivery of antitoxin to the remote town of Nome, Alaska, saved the town's children. It was carried 620 miles (1,000 kilometers) by dogsled in temperatures of –63°F (–53°C). The lead dog, Balto, is still considered a hero.

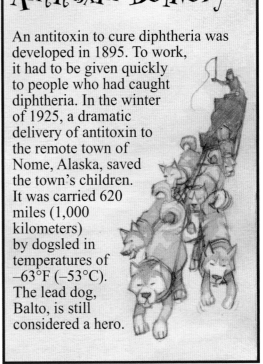

STRANGELY, poor people caught polio less often than rich people. It turned out that their drinking water was infected with the polio virus. They had developed a natural immunity to the disease by taking in small amounts.

DIPHTHERIA is caused by a toxin (poison) produced by a bacterium. The poison kills cells in the mouth and throat. Dead cells build up and block the throat, so victims find it difficult to breathe or swallow.

Let's Go For Herd Immunity

Mass vaccination creates "herd immunity" which protects everyone. When most people are immune to a disease, the few people who aren't immune are unlikely to come into contact with the disease, so even they are safe. But if not enough people are vaccinated, someone sick with the disease might meet an unprotected person—and then the disease can spread.

It's really important for everyone who can be vaccinated to do it—no freeloaders! Some people who are already sick or have a weak immune system can't be vaccinated. They depend on herd immunity, as do infants who are too young to get certain vaccines.

A SPECIAL NEEDLE with two points helped wipe out smallpox. It needed less vaccine for each patient.

The people colored red have not been vaccinated. But they are not likely to catch the disease, because most of the people they meet (blue lines) have been vaccinated.

Timeline:

1855: Smallpox vaccination made compulsory for schoolchildren in Massachusetts

1921: First mass vaccination program for diphtheria

In this group there are far more people who have not been vaccinated. They are likely to meet other unvaccinated people (red lines) and spread disease.

Top Tip

If you go abroad on vacation, you might need some extra shots to protect you from diseases that aren't common at home. In particular, you might need vaccination against tropical diseases. For malaria, there's no vaccine—you will need to take tablets.

IN ALL WARS before World War II, typhus ravaged troops. During World War II, a vaccine protected soldiers. Typhus is carried by lice that move between people in crowded, dirty conditions. It used to be common in jails and on ships. Soldiers often used to be more afraid of typhus than of enemy troops.

The Spread of Vaccination

1930s: Development of whooping cough vaccine

1962: First measles vaccine

1971: MMR triple vaccine for measles, mumps, and rubella

1955: Mass polio vaccination begins.

1969: Rubella vaccine

23

Vaccine Safety

Vaccines are given to millions of people to protect them, so it's vital that the vaccines themselves are safe to use. There are very strict rules to make sure new vaccines are safe—and that they work— before they are given to people. They are tested on cells, on animals, and on human volunteers before they are given to the public.

Vaccines are expensive to make and distribute. In countries where some people can't afford vaccines, aid programs pay for them. It helps all of us to reduce disease.

How Vaccines Are Made

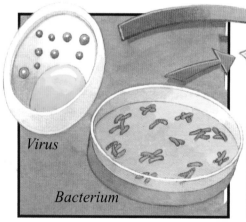

Virus

Bacterium

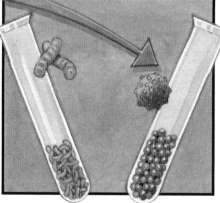

DON'T TRY THIS AT HOME! If the disease is bacterial, grow more bacteria on a plate of jelly with nutrients that the bacteria like. A virus can grow only inside a cell; grow it in an egg.

WHEN YOU HAVE ENOUGH, separate the bacteria or viruses from the jelly or egg. If you're making an inactivated vaccine, kill the viruses or bacteria with heat or chemicals.

AFTER ALL the processing to change your safe bacteria or virus into a vaccine, pack it into bottles and load it onto trucks for distribution. Remember to keep it cold.

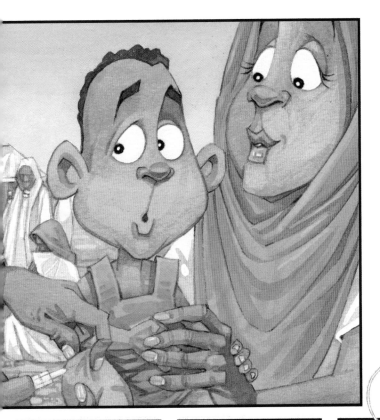

If you have a reaction to a vaccine, other than a sore arm or feeling slightly sick for a few hours, see a doctor. Vaccines are all tested for safety, but everyone's body is different, so it's best to check that you're okay.

I feel fine now.

SOMETIMES people feel sick after they have had a vaccination. Feeling a little achy or feverish for a short time is normal.

CHECK WITH A DOCTOR if you don't feel well—but it's usually just a coincidence if it comes after a vaccination.

IN 1998, a doctor published fake research saying the MMR vaccine was harmful. Fewer children were vaccinated as a result, and some died of measles.

VERY RARELY, someone has a serious reaction called anaphylactic shock after passive vaccination. They need medicine to get better.

Vaccination Challenges

There's still plenty for scientists working on vaccines to do. We have vaccines for 25 dangerous diseases, but some others are proving trickier to tackle.

We don't have a vaccine for malaria or HIV/AIDS, which both kill millions of people. Although we have flu vaccines, flu changes very quickly, so scientists need to keep changing the vaccine to keep up—with a new one each year. If a dangerous new flu virus emerges, it will take several months to make a vaccine for it. It's a race against time.

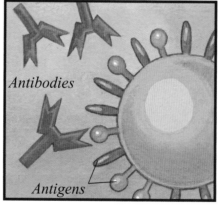

Antibodies

Antigens

WHEN an American soldier died of a new type of swine flu in 1976, people panicked. Was it about to kill millions, like the Spanish flu of 1918? No. A vaccine was rushed out, but the disease didn't spread. Fifteen people died from the vaccine and only one from flu. Unfortunately, it made people wary of vaccines.

THE FLU VIRUS can mutate (change) slowly, or suddenly if two types mix together. A new type of flu has different antigens on the surface, which don't match the antibodies we already have. Flu viruses can change and spread quickly, so it's a struggle to keep up. New flu strains are a big worry for scientists.

WHY ISN'T THERE a vaccine for everything? Some diseases change too quickly or come in too many different varieties for scientists to keep up. The common cold is one of those. It changes very quickly, and it's not very serious. It's better to spend effort combating more serious diseases.

IN 1918 a new type of flu called Spanish flu killed more than 50 million people worldwide. There was no vaccine against it.

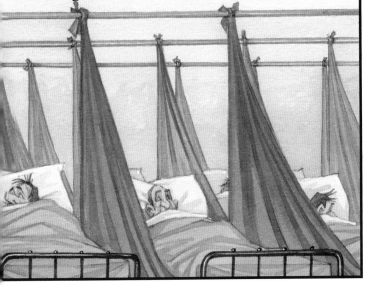

People who work with animals are the most likely source of a new mixed animal—human flu. If a farmer has human flu, and breathes in an animal-flu virus, the two viruses can join together. So keep away from that sneezing pig!

Snuffle

NOT ONLY PEOPLE get flu, and that's where the problems start. Most new forms of flu come from pigs or from birds such as chickens or ducks, but flu scientists are also keeping an eye on horses. Other animals can get flu, too: dogs, cats, seals, and whales all get flu.

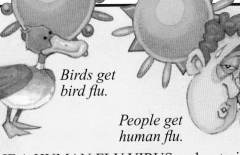

Birds get bird flu.

People get human flu.

IF A HUMAN FLU VIRUS and a strain of flu from an animal come together in the human body, the two types of flu virus can mix and match their parts, making a new, combined flu that humans can catch. Sometimes it's harmless, but it could be deadly. We don't have antibodies to fight the new flu, so it can spread quickly.

Bird flu + *Human flu* = *New flu*

Life Without Vaccination?

It's a little over 100 years since the first vaccines to prevent disease were developed. What would life be like without them now?

In the United States in 1952 there were 57,628 cases of polio, many of them children. Of those people, 3,145 died and 21,269 suffered permanent damage, with wasted limbs and paralysis. In 2013, there were no cases of polio in the United States—not one. Around the world, polio cases have fallen by 99% since 1988. There were about 200 cases in 2012, all in just three countries where polio hasn't quite been stamped out. So there is still more work to be done before everyone is safe.

THE POLIO VACCINE has saved around 10 million people from paralysis. That's 10 million people who can work and live active, independent lives, without pain.

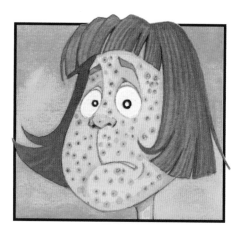

YOU WOULDN'T WANT to catch measles, but without vaccination, you probably would—it's one of the most infectious diseases of all. Without vaccination, 2.7 million people would die of measles each year.

WHOOPING COUGH is horrible. It can cause brain damage, seizures, and death. In the past, almost every child caught it. Countries that stop vaccinating have up to 100 times as many cases as those that keep vaccinating.

IN THE UNITED STATES, vaccination cut cases of diphtheria from 206,000 in 1921 to just 5 in the ten years from 2000 to 2010. The vaccination program broke down in the former Soviet Union, and 5,000 died from 1990 to 1999.

SMALLPOX has been wiped out in the wild—a victory for vaccination. But there are two samples in laboratories in the United States and Russia. Should we keep them for research, or get rid of them in case terrorists steal one?

SCIENTISTS are very close to a vaccine to stop you from eating too much! It speeds up the body's ability to burn calories.

Top Tip

Don't refuse vaccination—it's one of the greatest benefits of the modern world. It can save your life and protect other people around you. You wouldn't want to live without vaccination—and luckily you don't have to!

No More Needles?

THERE IS ALREADY a jet injector that forces the vaccine through the skin at high speed.

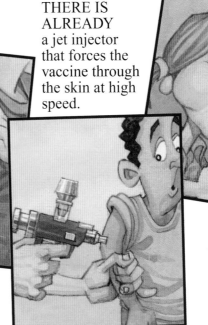

IN THE FUTURE, not all vaccines will come with a needle. Already, some can be sniffed as a nasal spray.

HOW ABOUT a stick-on patch, with microscopic needles you can barely feel?

ONE DAY, you might munch on a banana with a vaccine inside it. Don't eat the whole bunch!

Glossary

adaptive immunity The part of the immune system that produces antibodies for particular antigens.

anaphylactic shock A very strong allergic reaction. It can be fatal.

antibody A chemical made by the body that attaches to an antigen to help the immune system fight the antigen.

antigen Any substance that prompts the immune system to create antibodies.

antitoxin A chemical that combats the effects of a particular toxin (poison).

attenuated (or live) vaccine A vaccine made using a pathogen that has been altered to make it harmless.

bacteria Microscopic, single-celled organisms that sometimes cause disease.

cell The smallest building block of an organism that can reproduce by itself.

diphtheria A disease that causes cells in the mouth and throat to die and block up the airways.

epidemic A widespread outbreak of a disease.

genetic material The chemical DNA, which is found in cells and acts like a recipe for making an organism.

HIV/AIDS A viral disease that attacks the immune system.

immune system The body's system for fighting infection.

immunization Any method used to strengthen the body's immune system.

inactivated vaccine A vaccine made using a virus that has been killed.

infection The result of the body being attacked by pathogens that have entered the body and multiplied within it.

innate immune system The body's first response to infection, which is the same for any type of infection.

malaria A disease, caused by a microscopic parasite, that causes severe fever. It can be fatal.

microorganism A very small organism.

microscopic So small that it can be seen only by using a microscope.

MMR vaccine A vaccine that gives immunity to measles, mumps, and rubella.

mumps A viral disease that causes painful swelling of some glands.

organism Any living thing.

paralyzed Unable to move because of damage to muscles or nerves.

passive immunization Giving someone antibodies to combat a specific infection, rather than prompting their immune system to produce its own antibodies.

pathogen Something that causes a disease, such as a virus or bacterium.

phagocyte A type of white blood cell that destroys pathogens in the body.

polio A viral disease that can cause life-long paralysis and sometimes death.

protein A type of chemical that has many different roles within the body.

pustule A small, raised spot on the skin that contains pus (a yellowish fluid containing dead phagocytes).

rubella A viral disease (also called German measles) that is dangerous to pregnant women and their babies.

spinal cord The long bundle of nerve tissues that runs inside the vertebral column (backbone).

symptom A physical sign of disease, such as a rash, temperature, or vomiting.

typhus An often deadly bacterial disease that causes fever, back and joint pain, headaches, and confusion.

vaccine A substance given to prompt the body's immune system to make antibodies to fight a particular pathogen.

virus A fragment of genetic material in a protein casing that is on the borderline between living and nonliving things.

white blood cells (or leukocytes) Cells that are part of the body's immune system. Different types of white blood cells attack different pathogens.

Index

Top Vaccines

All countries have their own vaccination programs. Ask your doctor to make sure you've had all your shots. Here are nine important vaccinations, with descriptions of the diseases that they prevent.

. Diphtheria
Kills cells in the throat and blocks the airways. Kills around 10% of sufferers.

. Tetanus
Destroys the nerves and causes severe muscle spasms (tightening).

. Whooping cough
Very severe cough lasting six weeks, sometimes fatal.

. Meningitis
Attacks the membrane (thin layer of tissue) around the brain. Kills about half a million people a year worldwide.

5. Polio (poliomyelitis)
Attacks the nerves and can cause paralysis or death.

6. Hepatitis A and B
Attacks the liver and can cause death.

7. Rotavirus
Causes diarrhea leading to dehydration, killing nearly half a million children a year.

8. Measles/mumps/rubella (MMR)
Three diseases that can cause lasting harm, such as brain damage or damage to other organs.

9. Chickenpox
Causes an itchy rash and may lead to brain or lung damage.

Facts and Figures

Infectious diseases used to be a bigger problem than they are today. Vaccination in the United States, for example, has cut cases of 14 dangerous diseases by 90%, from about five and a half million to just under half a million a year.

But not everyone who is offered vaccination takes it. In the period 2007 to 2014, 140,000 people in the United States became sick with diseases that could have been prevented by vaccination — and 1,400 of them died. A serious reaction to a vaccine is extremely rare. The risk from a vaccine is many times less than the risk from the disease it protects you from.

This is what the great American statesman Benjamin Franklin wrote nearly 300 years ago:

"In 1736 I lost one of my Sons, a fine Boy of 4 Years old, taken by the Small Pox in the common way. I long regretted that I had not given it to him by Inoculation,* which I mention for the Sake of Parents, who omit that Operation on the Supposition that they should never forgive themselves if a Child died under it; my Example showing that the Regret may be the same either way, and that therefore the safer should be chosen."

Another name for variolation

Did You Know?

The human body can make hundreds of millions of different types of antibodies.

If you add together all the different types of living things on the planet, from tiny bacteria to humungous whales, there are more types of virus than all of them. There are (and have been) viruses to infect everything from bacteria, plants, and fungi to sharks and dinosaurs.

Two pints (one liter) of human blood contain about six billion phagocytes. There's an eager army ready to defend you!

The word *vaccine* comes from the Latin word *vaccinus*, which means "from the cow." It's called that because Jenner's first vaccine was made from cowpox which, obviously, comes from a cow!

- It's not just people who can be vaccinated. Farm animals are given vaccines to keep herds safe, and you can vaccinate your pet dog or cat, too. Even zoo animals are vaccinated. Would you want to stick a needle in an angry tiger? Well, zookeepers don't want to either, so they usually fire darts from a gun so that they don't have to get too close.